CEREMONIES and RITUALS

WORSHIP

BY JOANNA BRUNDLE

©2018
Book Life
King's Lynn
Norfolk PE30 4LS

ISBN: 978-1-78637-263-5

Written by:
Joanna Brundle

Edited by:
Kirsty Holmes

Designed by:
Daniel Scase

A catalogue record for this book
is available from the British Library.

CONTENTS

Words that look like **THIS** are explained in the glossary on page 31.

INTRODUCTION

Worship is the giving of praise and thanks to one God, to many gods and goddesses, or to spirits, according to the religious beliefs of the worshipper.

People worship in many different ways – alone, in small or large groups, at home or in places of worship such as a church or temple. Worship may be led by a religious teacher and follow a pattern with singing, prayers and RITUALS, or it may be the simple prayers of a family at a SHRINE at home. Whatever form it takes, true worship means that a person places their religion at the very centre of their life.

REASONS FOR WORSHIP

People worship for many reasons. They pray to serve their god, to offer thanks, to seek help and to ask for forgiveness for things they have done wrong, which are known as their sins. Worship gives people the chance to be part of a religious community and to praise their god in their thoughts, words and actions.

These children are praying quietly together. They have closed their eyes and put their hands together so that they can concentrate on their prayers.

These people are worshipping by singing hymns and raising their arms to God.

Saying thank you for the good things in our lives, such as sharing a family meal, is an important part of worship.

PILGRIMAGE

Some people offer worship by making a pilgrimage. This means they make a special journey to a **SACRED** place, such as the place of birth or death of a religious leader, or a place with special religious meaning. For followers of the Sikh faith, an important place of pilgrimage is the Harminder Sahib in Amritsar, India. It was founded in 1577 by **GURU** Ram Das and has over 39 million visitors each year.

The Harminder Sahib, known as The Golden Temple, is the most important temple or 'Gurdwara' in Sikhism.

THE GOLDEN TEMPLE

The Western Wall, the remains of an ancient Jewish temple destroyed by the Romans in A.D. 70, is an important place of worship for followers of Judaism.

SPIRIT WORSHIP

In some religions, people worship the spirits of their **ANCESTORS** or of the natural world. The Shinto religion of Japan, for example, is based on kami — spirits or gods of natural features such as mountains, seas and animals.

In some traditional cultures, people worship the spirit world, including the spirits of ancestors, to ask for fertile soil, sunshine and rain to grow crops, as well as protection from disease. Natural disasters, such as an earthquake, are seen as punishment from the gods.

NUNS AND MONKS

In many religions, there are people who decide to dedicate their whole lives to worship. They are known as nuns (female) or monks (male). They live in separate communities, leaving behind their possessions and families. They worship through prayer or **MEDITATION**, or by doing God's will through charity work.

Pilgrims climb to the summit of Mount Fuji to worship at the shrine of Sengen–Sama, goddess of growth and maturity.

ANCIENT WORSHIP RITUALS

Zeus was the god of the sky, and the king of the gods and goddesses on Mount Olympus.

THE ANCIENT GREEKS

The ancient Greeks worshipped 12 major gods and goddesses, who were believed to live on Mount Olympus. They believed that the gods and goddesses controlled everything in their lives. It was therefore very important to worship them to keep them happy – happy gods were helpful, but unhappy gods punished people. Offerings of wine, oil and milk were made and animals such as sheep and goats were sacrificed.

The gods and goddesses were believed to behave like adult humans – falling in love, arguing, having children and holding parties.

THE ROMANS

Temples for worship of the gods were built throughout the Roman Empire.

The remains of a Roman temple in Portugal dedicated to Diana, goddess of hunting.

Families also worshipped household spirits at home. Prayers to the gods were a trade-off – if the gods did what was asked of them (the nuncupatio), the worshippers promised to do something in return (the solutio). Offerings and sacrifices were made to persuade the gods to help. As the Empire grew, the Romans added gods from other cultures to their own. The gods of the Ancient Greeks all have Roman equivalents. Poseidon, for example, the Greek god of the sea, was known as Neptune by the Romans.

NEPTUNE

THE INCAS

The Inca civilisation thrived in coastal areas of the parts of South America now known as Peru and Chile from around A.D. 1200 to 1570. The Incas worshipped many gods and goddesses, believing that every mountain peak was either a god or was home to a god. The Sun-god, Inti, was believed to be the ancestor of the Inca people and worship of him was the basis of the Inca religion.

The Inti Raymi Sun festival is still held every year in Peru, to remember the importance of the Sun god Inti.

MACHU PICCHU

STONEHENGE

Stonehenge is a prehistoric MONUMENT in the U.K. It is a circle of huge standing stones, or monoliths, and is believed to have been a site of religious worship, especially of the Sun. Other examples of these stone circles were built across Europe from around 5000 to 1600 B.C. At the summer solstice, or longest day of the year, the central altar stone at Stonehenge lines up with the sunrise. Druids, followers of a spiritual religion known as Druidry, worship nature and still gather at Stonehenge to celebrate the sunrise at the summer solstice.

RUINS OF THE TEMPLE OF THE SUN

The 15th–century CITADEL of Machu Picchu in Peru, built for an Incan emperor, included the Temple of the Sun, or Torreón.

STONEHENGE

JUDAISM

Followers of Judaism, known as Jews, believe in one God who created the world. Jews worship at the synagogue, which is also a place of study and a community centre. Services at the synagogue can be led by a RABBI or by another member of the CONGREGATION. Traditionally, Jews should worship three times a day, in the morning, afternoon and evening. The Amidah is the central prayer of every Jewish worship service and is spoken whilst standing.

Ritual swaying from side to side, known as shuckling or shokeling, is a common practice for Jewish worshippers.

Singing is an important part of Jewish worship. Some synagogues have a cantor or hazzan – a professional singer, employed to lead the singing of prayers. Everyone (except unmarried women) wears a hat in the synagogue. They do this to show respect and reverence to God. Men wear a skull cap called a kippah. Women wear a hat or headscarf.

Jewish males usually begin wearing a kippah to attend the synagogue from the age of three.

INSIDE THE SYNAGOGUE

The Torah is the name given to the first five books of the Jewish bible. Jews believe that God gave the words of the Torah to the **PROPHET** Moses, and that it tells them how God wishes them to live. The words of the Torah are copied by hand onto **PARCHMENT**, which is rolled onto scrolls. The Torah is read during worship in the synagogue.

The reader of the Torah keeps their place in the text using a pointer known as a yad.

Every synagogue contains an Ark, which is a special cupboard, traditionally decorated with gold foil. The Ark contains the Torah Scrolls. It is named after the wooden chest containing the stone tablets given to Moses by God on Mount Sinai. These tablets were inscribed with the **TEN COMMANDMENTS**.

The Eternal Lamp, known as Ner Tamid, burns constantly and hangs above the Ark. It is a symbol of God's eternal presence and of the pillar of fire that guided the Jewish people out of slavery in Egypt.

During a service, the Ark is ceremonially opened and the Torah Scrolls are carried around the synagogue. The congregation normally stands whenever the doors of the Ark are open. As the Torah passes, worshippers touch it with their prayer shawl or prayer book. The Torah is read at a raised platform and desk called a bimah.

A BIMAH

THE TALLIT

Adult men often wear a prayer shawl known as a tallit for morning worship. A tallit has tassels around the edges. Looking at the tassels reminds the wearer to follow God's commandments.

A JEWISH WORSHIPPER WEARING HIS TALLIT FOR PRAYERS AT THE WESTERN WALL (SEE PAGE 5)

A ram's horn, known as a shofar, is blown at some synagogue services at special times of the year.

TEFILLIN

ORTHODOX Jews, wear tefillin on their head and arm during worship. Tefillin are small leather boxes containing texts from the Torah. Tefillin worn on the left arm close to the heart remind Jews to keep God's laws with all their heart. Tefillin worn on the forehead remind worshippers to concentrate on the teachings of the Torah with their whole mind.

A JEWISH WORSHIPPER WEARING TEFILLIN.

Tefillin have leather straps to hold them in place. The straps are wrapped around the arm and hand in a ritual pattern.

THE SABBATH

The Jewish Sabbath, or Shabbat, is the day of rest that begins at sundown on Friday evening and ends at sundown on Saturday. It is a day of worship, at home and at the synagogue, that begins when the whole family gathers for the Shabbat meal. Wine and plaited bread, called challah bread, are blessed and the meal itself becomes an act of worship, with the table serving as an altar.

CHALLAH BREAD, WINE AND CANDLES FOR THE SHABBAT MEAL

BAT MITZVAH AND BAR MITZVAH

Jewish girls and boys go through a **RITE OF PASSAGE** that marks the point in their lives when they become active members of the Jewish community. In a special ceremony at the synagogue, a girl becomes a Bat Mitzvah at 12 years old and a boy becomes a Bar Mitzvah at 13.

During the ceremony, children read from the Torah, watched by their family and friends. Afterwards, the family hosts a celebration meal or party at home.

A BAR MITZVAH CELEBRATION

Once they become a Bat or Bar Mitzvah, Jewish children are expected to follow God's commandments (mitzvot) and to behave responsibly.

SHAVU'OT

Jews celebrate Shavu'ot to remember the time when God gave the words of the Torah to Moses on Mount Sinai. God told Moses that the land promised to the Jews would be flowing with milk and honey. At Shavu'ot, Jews share a special meal containing these ingredients.

HONEY CAKE

Foods containing milk and honey are eaten at other Jewish celebrations too, including Rosh Hashanah (Jewish New Year).

SUKKOT

The Jewish festival of Sukkot lasts eight days. People build a hut, called a sukkah, at home or at the synagogue. Some live in the sukkah throughout the festival, while some just eat there. The sukkah reminds them that their ancestors lived in the open in the desert when they escaped slavery in Egypt.

Simhat Torah, meaning 'rejoicing in the Torah', is celebrated at the end of Sukkot. The Torah is carried around the synagogue, with joyful singing and dancing.

A sukkah usually has a roof made of palm leaves, so that the stars can be seen at night, just as they were in the desert.

CHRISTIANITY

CHRISTIAN WORSHIP IN CHURCH

Christians believe in one God. Their faith teaches them to love God and to follow the teachings of Jesus Christ, the Son of God. Christians worship God in different ways, with prayers, music, reading from the Bible and through holy ceremonies, known as SACRAMENTS.

Public worship with other Christians takes place in a church, chapel or CATHEDRAL. Christians believe that God always hears their prayers and can therefore be worshipped anywhere, at any time.

The word 'church' can mean the building in which worship takes place, or it can refer to the whole Christian community, also called 'the body of Christ'.

Christianity has many different groups, or denominations. Some, such as Anglicans, Roman Catholics and Orthodox Christians follow a set form of worship in church, called liturgical worship. They perform rituals and sacraments, which have special words and actions. Other denominations, such as Baptists, have no set form of worship and praise God in less formal ways. This is called non-liturgical worship. Whichever form it takes, public worship helps Christians to understand fully the importance of the Bible and of the life of Jesus.

These Christians are worshipping God by praying at home.

This choir from an orthodox church in Ethiopia is worshipping God with informal singing and playing of drums in an outdoor ceremony.

Some Christians, particularly Orthodox Christians, pray to religious icons – paintings or figures, often of Mary, Jesus, or his DISCIPLES.

ICON SHOWING JESUS AND HIS MOTHER MARY.

INSIDE A CHURCH

PULPIT

The pulpit is a raised platform where the priest gives his sermon – a talk, usually based on passages from the Bible.

STAINED GLASS

Stained glass windows often show Bible stories and were developed at a time when few people could read. The windows helped people to understand the Bible and gave them a focus for their worship.

PEWS

Worshippers used to stand or sit on straw-covered floors. Pews became common in the 16th century, when listening to preaching became popular. Hymn books may be left on the pews for worshippers to use during church services.

ALTAR

The altar is the holiest part of the church and is often separated from the rest of the church by a screen or railing. It is sometimes known as the Communion Table, because this is where the Eucharist is celebrated. (See page 14)

CROSS

Churches contain images of the cross, to remind worshippers of Jesus' **CRUCIFIXION**. Many churches are built in the shape of a cross and display a cross on the outside of the building and on the altar.

CANDLES

In the Bible, Jesus describes himself as 'the Light of the World'. Candles are lit in church to symbolise the light of Jesus. People also light candles to remember loved ones who have died.

VAULTED CEILING

Vaulted ceilings are arched ceilings that draw the attention of the congregation towards God and the heavens.

HOLY COMMUNION

The Bible teaches Christians that Jesus ate a meal, known as The Last Supper, with his disciples, before being crucified. Jesus shared bread and wine with them and told them to continue to do this, in memory of him. Holy Communion (also known as the Eucharist, Mass or the Lord's Supper) is celebrated in church to remember Jesus and that he died to pay for humanity's sins. Christians say sorry to God for things they have done wrong and are offered a small piece of bread and a sip of wine, that represent the body and blood of Jesus.

Some Christian groups, including Roman Catholics, believe that the bread and wine actually become the body and blood of Jesus during the Eucharist ceremony.

FIRST COMMUNION AND CONFIRMATION

First Communion and Confirmation are ceremonies that take place in some Christian churches. First Communion is the first time that a child receives the Eucharist. In the Catholic Church, boys and girls receive their First Communion at the age of seven or eight, but children can be older or younger in other denominations. The Confirmation ceremony enables Christians to become full members of the Christian community and to confirm the promises made for them, when they were baptised as babies.

CHILDREN CELEBRATING THEIR FIRST COMMUNION IN A GREEK ORTHODOX CHURCH

The white clothes traditionally worn by boys and girls symbolise purity.

A CONFIRMATION CEREMONY IN FINLAND

During the Confirmation ceremony, baptised Christians confirm that they believe in God, Jesus and the Holy Spirit and reject evil.

CHRISTIAN CELEBRATIONS

Easter marks Jesus' death and his return to life in the **RESURRECTION**. During the week leading up to Easter, known as Holy Week, processions take place in Orthodox and Catholic countries. On Easter Sunday, joyful services of worship are held and churches are filled with flowers.

AN EASTER PROCESSION IN SPAIN, SHOWING JESUS RIDING ON A DONKEY

CHRISTMAS

At Christmas, Christians celebrate the birth of Jesus Christ. Advent is the period covering the four Sundays leading up to Christmas when Christians prepare for this important time. An Advent ring is placed in church, and candles are lit each Sunday, one on the first Sunday of Advent, two on the second and so on. The central candle is lit on Christmas Day.

POPE FRANCIS CELEBRATING MASS AT THE VATICAN, ROME

The exact date of Jesus' birth is not known. The date we know as Christmas Day, 25th December, was chosen around A.D. 336 to fall at the same time as a PAGAN festival for Mithra, god of light.

A model of the stable where Jesus was born is set up in church but the figure of Jesus is not added until Christmas Day.

AN ADVENT RING, WITH ALL THE CANDLES LIT FOR CHRISTMAS DAY

Epiphany is celebrated on 6th January to honour the coming of the three kings (shown on the right of the scene) to baby Jesus.

Churches are beautifully decorated with flowers and candles for Christmas Day, when services of worship and thanksgiving take place. Carols are sung and the story of Jesus' birth is read aloud from the Bible.

A Christmas service in an Orthodox church in Ukraine.

ISLAM

Followers of Islam are known as Muslims. Muslims worship together at a mosque. As well as being a house of worship, a mosque is also a place to study and to celebrate festivals, such as RAMADAN. Muslims don't have to attend the mosque to pray – they can pray anywhere, provided it is clean.

Muslims pray five times a day, reciting daily prayers in ARABIC: at dawn, just after noon, mid-afternoon, just after sunset and after dark. The prayers are mostly verses from the Qur'an, the Muslim holy book. Extra prayers can be said at any time.

Some Muslims use prayer beads to help them to concentrate on their prayers. The 99 beads remind Muslims of the 99 names of Allah.

Allah is the Muslim name for God.

FRIDAY PRAYERS AT A MOSQUE IN MALAYSIA

THE CALL TO PRAYER

The call to prayer, the Adhan, goes out from the mosque at five set times each day. Verses from the Sunnah (writings that speak of the deeds and words of Allah) are recited by the mu'adhin, or muezzin, usually using a loudspeaker system. All male Muslims must attend mid–day prayers at the mosque on Fridays. Prayers are led by the IMAM.

The word 'imam' comes from Arabic words meaning 'leader of the way'.

THE CALL TO PRAYER

Cleanliness is an important part of Islamic prayer. Wudu is ritual washing that Muslims perform before prayer and before handling and reading the Qur'an. It involves washing the hands, mouth, nostrils, arms, head and feet with water, whilst saying special prayers.

Mosques have special areas, with taps and seating, set aside for wudu.

On entering the mosque, Muslims take off their shoes. Inside the prayer hall, they say prayers together. Muslims believe that peace comes from complete obedience to the will of Allah. The prayers involve recitations from the Qur'an and ritual movements of the body, including bowing, standing and kneeling, that show this obedience. The words and movements follow a precise order. After the group prayers, Muslims may offer their own, personal prayers called du'a. Worship at the mosque does not include any music or singing.

Prostration – praying with the forehead, knees, hands and feet touching the floor – shows that Muslims submit to the will of Allah.

Women are allowed to attend the mosque, but usually sit separately from the men. They must cover their heads for prayer.

The Ka'bah is a black cube–shaped building at the centre of the Masjid al-Haram, the Great Mosque of Mecca.

FACING MECCA

Mecca, or Makkah, is the city in Saudi Arabia where the prophet **MUHAMMAD** was born. When they pray, Muslims must face towards the Ka'bah at Mecca, the most sacred Islamic place on Earth. Inside every mosque, there is a semi-circular niche, known as a mihrab, in the prayer wall or qiblah. The mihrab shows Muslims the direction they should face.

Outside the mosque, worshippers use a compass to tell them the direction of Mecca. Some prayer mats have a built-in compass for this purpose.

THE BLUE MOSQUE IN ISTANBUL, TURKEY

INSIDE A MOSQUE

Although there are many different styles of mosque, depending on the **ARCHITECTURE** of the country, all mosques share some common features. As well as the mihrab, most have at least one minaret; a tall tower that is the highest point of the mosque. It is traditionally used for calling Muslims to prayer.

Mosques usually have one, two or four minarets. The Blue Mosque in Istanbul is unusual because it has six minarets.

Mosques are sometimes decorated with crescents and stars, the symbols of Islam.

Most mosques also have a dome-shaped roof. The dome is often directly above the prayer hall, which is carpeted.

The Central Mosque in London, England, has a golden dome.

The prayer hall has no furniture, so that worshippers have room to perform the ritual movements of worship. During Friday prayers, the imam gives a sermon, known as the khutba, from the minbar, a raised pulpit.

The geometric mosaic decorations are a common feature of mosques.

There are never any pictures or statues of people or animals in the mosque, because Muslims must avoid the sin of idolatry, known as shirk. Shirk means worshipping something other than Allah. Allah is considered to be beyond human understanding, so there are no images of him, or of the prophet Muhammad, inside the mosque either.

THE FIVE PILLARS OF ISLAM

The Five Pillars of Islam tell Muslims how to follow their religion correctly. They are:

- The Shahada – the declaration of faith
- Salam – daily prayers
- Zukah – giving to charity
- Sawm – **FASTING** during Ramadan
- Hajj – pilgrimage to Mecca

All healthy Muslim men and women are expected to make the pilgrimage, which takes place during the twelfth Muslim month, at least once in their lifetime. Over two million pilgrims make the journey each year. They wear simple white clothes, symbolising that everyone is equal in the eyes of Allah.

During Hajj, pilgrims perform tawaf. This ritual that involves walking around the Ka'bah seven times in an anti–clockwise direction.

The purpose of Hajj is to strengthen the pilgrim's faith, to give them peace in their soul, and to make them a better person.

EID AL-ADHA

Eid al-Adha marks the end of the Hajj and is one of the holiest days of the Islamic year. The festival remembers the obedience of **IBRAHIM** who was willing to sacrifice his son to God. God eventually gave Ibrahim a ram to sacrifice instead.

Muslims thank God for his mercy to Ibrahim by sharing a whole sheep or goat with family, friends and the poor.

EID UL-FITR

Eid ul-Fitr is a joyful festival at the end of Ramadan, when families share their first meal during daylight for a month. It is a time of celebration and happiness, with special prayers of thanksgiving at the mosque. Presents are given, symbolising the blessings that will come to Allah's followers.

Traditional foods for the Eid ul-Fitr celebrations include sweet dishes, like these Eid cookies.

HINDUISM

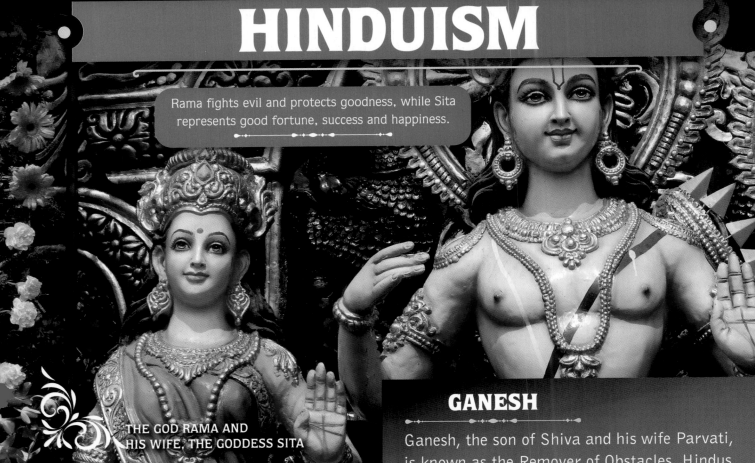

Rama fights evil and protects goodness, while Sita represents good fortune, success and happiness.

THE GOD RAMA AND HIS WIFE, THE GODDESS SITA

Followers of Hinduism worship many gods and goddesses, but they believe that all these DEITIES are different forms of the one supreme God, known as Brahman. The main Hindu deities, known as The Trimurti, are: Brahma the creator, Vishnu the great preserver, and Shiva the destroyer and recreator.

Although Hinduism has thousands of deities, Hindus can choose which ones they will worship. Sometimes, they are chosen because they have particular qualities that appeal to the worshipper. Families often pray to deities that have had special importance for them.

GANESH

Ganesh, the son of Shiva and his wife Parvati, is known as the Remover of Obstacles. Hindus often pray to him before beginning anything new, such as a journey. It is said that, having accidentally beheaded his son, Shiva promised to replace his head with that of the first creature he saw, which was an elephant! Ganesh is always shown with a large pot-belly that symbolises success and wealth.

The celebration of Ganesh Chaturthi is a ten–day festival for the worship of Ganesh.

PUJA

Puja is the name given to daily Hindu worship, which can take place either at home or at a Hindu temple, known as a mandir. Hindus believe that God is everywhere and so they can worship anywhere, at any time. Most Hindu families set up a shrine at home. The shrine is decorated with pictures and statuettes called murtis, of the family's favourite gods.

To symbolise spiritual wisdom, a Hindu worshipper may make a mark on their forehead, called a tilak. Sandalwood paste, known as kum kum, is used for this purpose.

A symbol of the sacred sound 'Om' may be kept at the shrine.

Hindus begin puja by making the sound 'Om', the sacred sound representing Brahman.

Other MANTRAS from the scriptures are then recited. The murti of the god is treated like a guest and may be washed, decorated and offered gifts including flowers and food. Worshippers take turns to pass a lit lamp around the murtis and ask for blessings. They quickly pass their hands over the flame and then put their hands to their head to receive the gods' blessings. This is called the Arti ceremony.

Puja should involve the whole person in worship, so the shrine includes items that reach all the human senses: a bell is rung to focus the mind and sweet-smelling INCENSE may be burnt.

Boys go through a samskar – a rite of passage – known as Upanayana or The Sacred Thread Ceremony, after which they are allowed to help in puja at home and to read the sacred texts, the Vedas. Three cotton threads are placed over the shoulder, symbolising respect for god and their parents.

MEMBERS OF A HINDU FAMILY PERFORMING PUJA AT HOME.

WORSHIP AT THE MANDIR

There are many different murtis at the mandir. They are usually elaborately decorated. Public worship at the mandir is similar to worship at home but is led by a Brahmin, a Hindu priest. The Brahmin chants mantras and reads from the sacred texts. Before worship, Hindus carry out cleansing rituals. They remove their shoes, wash their feet and rinse their mouth, before making offerings to their chosen god. The holiest part of the mandir is the garbhagriha. It houses the murti of the main deity of the temple. Only the priest is allowed to enter this sacred space.

The gopura, or tower, of this mandir in India is beautifully decorated with different murtis.

PILGRIMAGE

Hindus consider pilgrimage to be an important act of worship. The Indian city of Varanasi, also known as the City of Light, stands on the banks of the River Ganges. It is a favourite place for pilgrimage because it is considered to be the home of Shiva. Ganga, the goddess of rivers, has given her name to the River Ganges. It is considered by Hindus to be the most sacred of all rivers. Bathing in the Ganges, especially at Varanasi, has special importance for Hindus.

HINDU WOMEN BATHING IN THE RIVER GANGES AT VARANASI

Water taken from the River Ganges is used all over the world in ceremonies and rituals of worship.

HINDU FESTIVALS

The five-day festival of Diwali is known as the Festival of Lights. Hindus invite Lakshmi, the goddess of wealth and good fortune, into their homes by lighting divas (small oil lamps). Using coloured rice powder, they make special decorations called rangoli patterns on the floor at the entrance to the home.

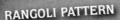
RANGOLI PATTERN

KRISHNA JANMASHTAMI

This festival celebrates the birthday of Krishna, one of the most commonly worshipped Hindu gods.

Children are dressed as Krishna and other gods in this street parade celebrating Krishna Janmashtami.

At the mandir, religious songs known as kirtan are sung through the day and there are readings from the Bhagavad Gita, the Hindu scripture. Krishna was born at midnight, so at this time, a crib containing an image of him is rocked. Offerings of dairy products, such as butter, are made to remember Krishna's work as a cowherd.

The orange pot hanging in the air is filled with butter. The young men have formed to human tower to reach and break the butter pot, to remember Krishna's time as a cowherd.

SIKHISM

Followers of Sikhism are known as Sikhs. Sikhism was founded in AD 1500 by Guru Nanak. Most Sikhs live in India but the religion has spread all around the world.

Sikh beliefs were passed on through a series of nine further gurus, the last of whom was Guru Gobind Singh (1666–1708). He decided that, after his death, the Sikh holy book, the Guru Granth Sahib, would act as the final guru for the Sikh people. For this reason, it is always shown the same respect that would be shown to a human guru.

The Guru Granth Sahib contains the teachings and poetry of the ten gurus.

For Sikhs, worship is a very important part of their lives. Sikhs worship one true God, referred to as Waheguru, who is the creator of everything in the universe.

The opening words of the Guru Granth Sahib are 'God is One, He is the True Name, He is the Creator'.

THE GURDWARA

A Sikh temple is called a Gurdwara, which means 'door to the Guru'. Any building that contains a copy of the Guru Granth Sahib is considered to be a Gurdwara. Some are very simple while others are very large and elaborately decorated.

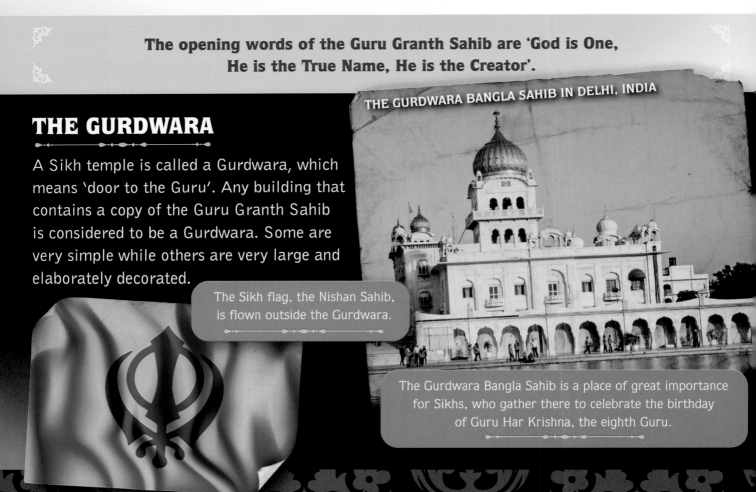

THE GURDWARA BANGLA SAHIB IN DELHI, INDIA

The Sikh flag, the Nishan Sahib, is flown outside the Gurdwara.

The Gurdwara Bangla Sahib is a place of great importance for Sikhs, who gather there to celebrate the birthday of Guru Har Krishna, the eighth Guru.

INSIDE THE GURDWARA

Sikhs do not have images of God in the Gurdwara because they do not consider God to have any form humans can recognise. Worship takes place in a prayer hall, called a diwan, meaning 'court of a ruler'. The Guru Granth Sahib is carried into the diwan each morning. It is placed on top of a cushion on a takht, which is a raised platform with a canopy.

The Guru Granth Sahib is underneath the golden canopy.

INSIDE THE GURDWARA SIS GANI SAHIB IN DELHI, INDIA.

During readings, a chauri (whisk) is waved over the Guru Granth Sahib, to show respect and honour. When it is not being read, the Holy Book is covered by beautiful silk cloths called rumalas. At night, it is carefully put away into its own special room.

A traditional chauri is made from yak or goat hair or from peacock feathers.

A GRANTHI (SIKH RELIGIOUS TEACHER) READING FROM THE GURU GRANTH SAHIB

A RAGI PLAYING THE TABLA

Music and singing are very important features of Sikh worship. Hymns, known as shabads, from the Holy Book are sung during services. Musicians called ragis accompany the singing, usually playing the harmonium and a pair of drums called tabla.

The ragis usually sit on the floor to play their instruments.

A harmonium is a small, portable keyboard instrument, rather like an organ.

25

THE GURDWARA

There is no set day for worship, but a Sunday service is usually held at the Gurdwara. Before entering the diwan, Sikhs wash, remove their shoes and cover their heads. They then bow down in front of the Guru Granth Sahib, as a sign of respect.

VOLUNTEERS HELPING TO PREPARE FOOD IN THE LANGAR

Worshippers make an offering of money or food to support the langar, the kitchen and dining area of the Gurdwara, where free meals (also called langar) are offered to all people, whatever their religion or background.

Worshippers sit on the floor. They face the Holy Book and must not turn their backs towards it. Men and women usually sit separately. Although there are no priests in Sikhism, every Gurdwara has a Granthi. He reads from the Guru Granth Sahib and leads prayers, including the Ardas prayer, which asks God to bless Sikhs. After the service, everyone shares karah parshad, a sweet treat. Eating together shows that everyone is part of the Sikh family and equal in God's eyes.

Helping others and sharing are important parts of Sikh worship.

THE AMRIT CEREMONY

Teenage Sikh boys and girls can decide for themselves whether they wish to become full members of the Sikh faith. The Amrit Ceremony confirms Sikhs as full members of their religion. It takes place at the Gurdwara. During the ceremony, amrit is drunk five times and is sprinkled in the eyes and on the head.

Amrit is a mixture of sugar and water that has been stirred with a double-edged sword called a khanda and blessed with prayers.

KHANDA

THE AMRIT CEREMONY

Sikhs celebrate the lives of the ten Gurus with festivals known as gurpurabs. A non-stop reading of the Guru Granth Sahib, called the Arkand Path, takes place at the Gurdwara, finishing on the day of the festival. It takes 48 hours to complete and people take it in turns to read. The Gurdwara is decorated with flowers, flags and lights. Sikhs dress in smart new clothes and come to the Gurdwara, to take part in special services that include hymns sung from the Guru Granth Sahib. Outside some Gurdwaras, sweets are offered to everyone, whatever their faith.

Gurpurabs are often marked with street parades, involving dancing, singing and beating of drums.

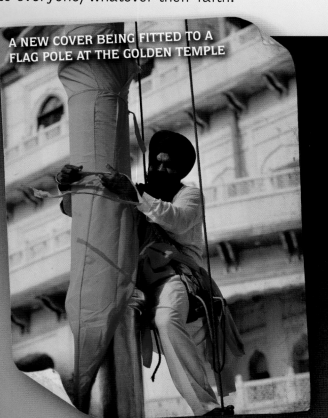

A NEW COVER BEING FITTED TO A FLAG POLE AT THE GOLDEN TEMPLE

BAISAKHI

Baisakhi (also known as Vaisakhi) is one of the most important Sikh religious festivals. It celebrates Guru Gobind Singh who founded the Sikh community, known as the Khalsa, in 1699. It is also the time when Sikhs celebrate the harvest and their new year. At the Gurdwara, a ceremony takes place in which the flagpole is taken down and cleaned. The cover and the flag itself are replaced with new ones.

SIKHS TAKING PART IN A BAISAKHI PARADE IN ITALY

Yellow and orange are the traditional colours of Baisakhi, because Guru Gobind Singh said that Sikhs should brighten the world with joyful colours.

Baisakhi is celebrated all over the world with street processions known as nagar kirtan. Shabads are sung through the streets, to involve the whole community in worship.

BUDDHISM

Buddhism was founded around 2,500 years ago by a prince, Siddhartha Gautama, who gave up his riches and family to seek the meaning of life. He eventually understood that true happiness comes when people are content with what they have. This understanding is known as enlightenment.

Siddhartha Gautama became known as the Buddha after his enlightenment. 'Buddha' means 'enlightened one'.

The bump on top of the Buddha's head shows that he had special talents. The round mark on his forehead is his third eye, to see things others cannot see.

Buddhists do not think of the Buddha as a god. They show him respect and thanks by meditating, praying and studying his teachings. A place where an image of the Buddha is used for worship is known as a shrine. Buddhists may worship at a shrine set up at home or they may visit a temple or **VIHARA** to worship with others. Worshippers burn incense and decorate their shrines with offerings of flower garlands.

FLOWER GARLAND, INCENSE STICKS

The Shanti Stupa in northern India contains relics of the Buddha at its base. It was built to celebrate 2,500 years of Buddhism.

STUPAS

Buddhists also worship by visiting stupas, which are burial mounds or shrines containing **RELICS** of the Buddha or other religious teachers. Worshippers walk around the stupa, reciting mantras and prayers.

WORSHIP AT THE TEMPLE

The shrine room is the most important part of the temple and contains one or more images of the Buddha.

Images of the Buddha are always placed at a higher level than that of the congregation, to show respect for the Buddha and his enlightenment.

Worshippers must take off their shoes before entering, as a mark of respect and to keep the shrine clean. They wear modest clothing and bow in front of the Buddha before sitting or kneeling for worship.

Buddhist worshippers sit with their feet tucked under as it is considered disrespectful to point the soles of the feet towards the Buddha.

Worship in the temple is usually led by a monk, but nuns or other respected Buddhists can lead the worship too. Within Buddhism, there are different ways of worshipping but usually, there is chanting of mantras and verses from the scriptures. Some Buddhists chant in their own language but others use Pali or Sanskrit, ancient Indian languages. Some spin a prayer wheel, containing prayers and mantras, as they are chanting. They believe that the prayer is repeated each time the wheel turns. Some write prayers on colourful flags, which are hung up on lines at places of worship. The worshippers believe that the prayer is repeated each time the flag blows in the wind.

THE MAHABODHI TEMPLE IN INDIA MARKS THE PLACE OF THE BUDDHA'S ENLIGHTENMENT.

A PRAYER WHEEL

PRAYER FLAGS AT A STUPA IN NEPAL

Dana is a special service that is held at the vihara every morning. Different parts of the Buddha's teachings, such as the importance of kindness to others, are covered at each Dana ceremony.

BUDDHIST MONKS

Any community of Buddhist nuns or monks is known as a sangha. After his enlightenment, the Buddha formed the first sangha of monks who heard his first sermon. In Buddhist Thailand, it is still a common practice for boys to spend some time living as a monk, to help them to understand the teachings of the Buddha. A Buddhist monk lives a simple life, with very few possessions other than robes and a begging bowl.

The begging bowl has a lid, used as a plate.

A BUDDHIST MONK MEDITATING

Buddhist monks try not to harm any living thing, however small, and are allowed to own a water strainer so that they don't swallow an insect by accident! They seek perfect inner peace by meditating.

The legs are always crossed, the hands are folded and the eyes are closed to shut out any distractions.

The Ajanta caves in India were formed around 2,000 years ago and were used by Buddhist monks as a place of worship. Murals on the cave walls show scenes from the Buddha's life.

VESAK

Vesak, also known as Wesak, is a festival to celebrate the Buddha's birth, enlightenment and death. Buddhists visit the temple, to pray and to listen to lectures about the Buddha's life and teachings. They decorate their homes with coloured lanterns and enjoy a feast with family and friends.

A monk blesses worshippers with holy water as they pray to the Buddha during Vesak celebrations in Indonesia.

GLOSSARY

ancestors	people from whom a person is descended
Arabic	traditionally, the language of the Arab people, now commonly used in North Africa and parts of Asia
architecture	a style or method of building
cathedral	the most important Christian church in an area, usually associated with a bishop
citadel	a fortress, usually built on high ground, protecting a city
congregation	a group of people who have come together in a religious building for worship
crucifixion	being killed on a cross
deities	gods or goddesses
disciples	followers of Jesus
fasting	going without food
guru	religious or spiritual teacher
Ibrahim	a Muslim prophet
imam	a religious teacher in the Islamic faith
incense	a spice that is burned to produce a sweet smell
mantras	words or phrases repeated many times by people who are praying or meditating
meditation	the act of thinking and concentrating deeply, whilst being calm and still
monument	an ancient building or other construction that has been preserved
Muhammad	the founder of the Islamic faith, to whom God's word was revealed
orthodox	a follower of a religion who adheres exactly to its rules and practices
pagan	a traditional religion based on reverence for nature
parchment	a stiff, thin flat writing material, prepared from the skin of animals such as sheep
prophet	a messenger or teacher of the will of God
rabbi	a teacher of Judaism
Ramadan	the month–long Islamic festival when Muslims do not eat during daylight hours
relics	objects with great religious meaning or the remains of a saint or holy person or of their possessions
Resurrection	Jesus' return to life from death after being crucified on the cross
rite of passage	an important event, particularly a religious event, in a person's life
rituals	solemn or religious ceremonies with a series of actions carried out in a strict order
sacraments	religious ceremonies or rituals
sacred	connected to a god or gods
shrine	a holy place or a place of worship, often marked by a building or other construction or a structure containing a sacred object
Ten Commandments	God's rules for how people should live, given to Moses on Mount Sinai
vihara	a Buddhist temple or monastery

INDEX

PHOTO CREDITS